260L

KING ARTHUR

A GRAPHIC CLASSIC BY
TERRY M. WEST

BASED ON THE STORY
"THE SWORD IN THE STONE"

LANE

FORT WAYNE COMMUNITY SCHOOLS
Fort Wayne, Indiana

SCHOLASTIC INC.
New York Toronto London Auckland Sydney
Mexico City New Delhi Hong Kong

PENCILLER
MICHAEL LILLY

INKER
SCOTT GOODELL

COLORIST
J. BROWN AND TECH FX

LETTERER
FRED VAN LENTE

COVER ARTIST
MICHAEL LILLY

COVER COLORS
J. BROWN AND TECH FX

20 19 18 17 16 15 14 13   7 8 9/0

KING ARTHUR

STORYTELLERS HAVE BEEN TALKING ABOUT KING ARTHUR FOR MORE THAN 1,000 YEARS.

ARTHUR, THEY SAY, WAS THE GREATEST RULER ENGLAND EVER HAD. HE LIVED IN A HUGE CASTLE CALLED CAMELOT.

THERE, HE MET WITH HIS BRAVE KNIGHTS. THEY PLANNED DANGEROUS TRIPS TO PROTECT THEIR LAND FROM EVIL KNIGHTS AND HORRIBLE MONSTERS.

MERLIN THE WIZARD WAS ANOTHER IMPORTANT CHARACTER AT CAMELOT. MERLIN USED HIS MAGIC POWERS TO PROTECT ARTHUR. "THE SWORD IN THE STONE" TELLS THE STORY OF THE FIRST TIME MERLIN HELPED ARTHUR.

A LONG TIME AGO, KING UTHER WAS THE LEADER OF ENGLAND. HE WAS A GOOD RULER, BUT THE DAY CAME WHEN HE DIED. THERE WERE RUMORS THAT HE HAD A SON. BUT NO SON COULD BE FOUND. THERE WAS NO PRINCE TO TAKE UTHER'S PLACE.

SOON, UTHER'S KNIGHTS STARTED FIGHTING OVER WHO WOULD BE KING. ENGLAND BECAME A DANGEROUS PLACE....

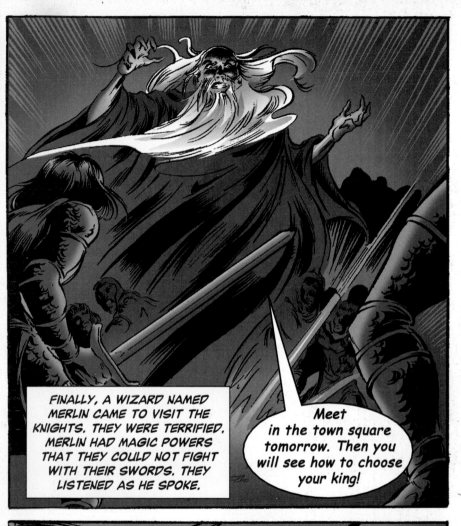

FINALLY, A WIZARD NAMED MERLIN CAME TO VISIT THE KNIGHTS. THEY WERE TERRIFIED. MERLIN HAD MAGIC POWERS THAT THEY COULD NOT FIGHT WITH THEIR SWORDS. THEY LISTENED AS HE SPOKE.

Meet in the town square tomorrow. Then you will see how to choose your king!

THE NEXT MORNING, THE KNIGHTS MET IN THE SQUARE. THEY SAW A LARGE STONE WITH A SWORD STICKING OUT OF IT. THEY READ WHAT WAS WRITTEN ON THE STONE.

ALL OF THE KNIGHTS TRIED, BUT NO ONE COULD FREE THE SWORD.

FOR 13 YEARS, THE SWORD STAYED IN THE STONE. MANY PEOPLE TRIED TO PULL IT FREE. BUT NO ONE COULD.

THEY RODE TOWARD THE CASTLE. ECTOR WAS WORRIED THAT THEY WOULD NOT BE ABLE TO FIND A PLACE TO STAY.

There will be many people at the contests tomorrow. I hope we'll be able to find an inn.

I could ride ahead and find us a room.

All right. See if you can find a place for us. Then meet us in the town square.

Whoever wins the contests tomorrow will get a chance to pull the sword from the stone.

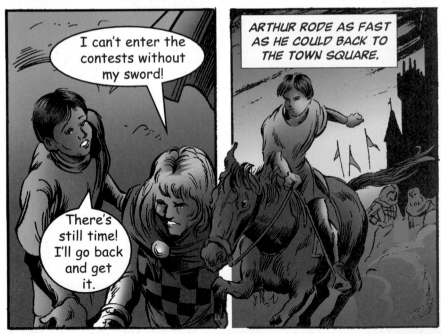

ARTHUR RETURNED AS QUICKLY AS HE COULD. HE HOPED THERE WAS STILL TIME TO GET THE SWORD TO KAY.

I'm back!

It's about time!

It's not your sword. The inn was locked. I found this sword in the square.

What?! But I wanted my ...

... sword....

I have always known that you would become king, Arthur.

You see, you are not my son.

What?

Call him Arthur.

"RIGHT BEFORE KING UTHER DIED, MERLIN CAME TO MY HOME. HE WAS CARRYING YOU IN HIS ARMS. HE TOLD ME TO TAKE CARE OF YOU. KING UTHER KNEW THE KINGDOM OF ENGLAND WAS FALLING APART. HE HAD MANY ENEMIES. HE WANTED HIS SON TO STAY IN A SAFE PLACE."

I knew this day would come. I will miss you, my son.